Robert Maass

When Autumn Comes

OCT 2 2 2016

Henry Holt and Company
NEW YORK

Henry Holt and Company, LLC, *Publishers since 1866*
115 West 18th Street, New York, New York 10011

Henry Holt is a registered
trademark of Henry Holt and Company, LLC

Distributed in Canada by H. B. Fenn and Company Ltd.

Library of Congress Cataloging-in-Publication Data
Maass, Robert.
When autumn comes / by Robert Maass.
Summary: Depicts in words and photographs the coming of autumn.
1. Autumn—Juvenile literature. [1. Autumn.] I. Title.
QB637.7.M3   1990   508—dc20   90-32069

ISBN 0-8050-2349-6
First published in hardcover in 1990 by Henry Holt and Company
First Owlet paperback edition—1992
Printed in Hong Kong

13   15   14

When summer ends and autumn comes,
it's time to put on sweaters and long pants.

Birds fly south to warmer places.

Boats are pulled up onto shore.

School has just begun
when autumn comes.
Old friends are together
and new friends are made.

Autumn is a time for making ready—for painting

and fixing

and changing
and airing.

It's a time
of preparation.

Wood is cut,
gathered,
and stacked in cords.

A chimney sweep
brushes away soot
inside the chimney
so fires will burn well.

Leaves turn red,
orange, yellow, brown,
painting the ground
as they fall.
They're raked up
so grass can grow
in the spring,
and to make great
jumping-into piles.

The farmer knows
that autumn's here.
He reaps and threshes
and stores the
late feed corn.
Lambs' woolly coats
grow thick.

Apples ripen.
Cider is pressed

and taken home.

Indian corn decorates
the season.
Pumpkins are harvested
from the fields.
Halloween is coming soon.

Pumpkin people
spring up on lawns.
It's time to dress up,
trick-or-treat,
and be spooky.

Days grow shorter
and shadows stretch.
By now there are just
a few more nuts to store.

When the first
frost comes,
the cold
is easy to see.

At Thanksgiving, families gather to feast
and to remember the good things of the year.

Then caps and boots and heavy coats are taken out.
Winter's at our heels

12 05

as autumn ends.